Goodwill Impairment Essentials

Steven M. Bragg

AccountingTools®

ISBN 978-1-64221-318-8

For more information about AccountingTools® products, visit our Web site at www.accountingtools.com.

Table of Contents

About the Author

Steven Bragg, CPA, has been the chief financial officer or controller of four companies, as well as a consulting manager at Ernst & Young. He received a master's degree in finance from Bentley College, an MBA from Babson College, and a Bachelor's degree in Economics from the University of Maine. He has been a two-time president of the Colorado Mountain Club, and is an avid alpine skier, mountain biker, and certified master diver. Mr. Bragg resides in Centennial, Colorado. He has written more than 300 books and courses, including *New Controller Guidebook*, *GAAP Guidebook*, and *Payroll Management*.

Steven maintains the accountingtools.com web site, which contains continuing professional education courses, the Accounting Best Practices podcast, and thousands of articles on accounting subjects.

Buy Additional AccountingTools Courses

AccountingTools offers more than 1,500 hours of CPE courses, with concentrations in accounting, auditing, finance, taxation, and ethics. Related courses that you might like include:

- Intangible Assets
- Intangible Asset Valuation
- Mergers and Acquisitions

Go to accountingtools.com/cpe to view these additional courses.

AccountingTools®

Goodwill Impairment Essentials

Introduction

This manual is designed to give the reader a solid understanding of the accounting for goodwill impairment. The reporting requirements for goodwill impairment are stated in detail in Topic 350-20 of the Accounting Standards Codification, as promulgated by the Financial Accounting Standards Board (FASB). The manual also covers the related financial statement disclosure and presentation requirements, as well as the goodwill amortization option.

The Nature of Goodwill

Goodwill is a common byproduct of a business combination, where the purchase price paid for the acquiree is higher than the fair values of the identifiable assets and liabilities acquired. In this situation, the goodwill intangible asset is recorded on the books of the acquiring entity, and represents the future economic benefits arising from unidentified assets that have been acquired in a business combination. When goodwill is initially recognized, it is measured by the acquirer as of the date when it acquires the target business.

In brief, goodwill is calculated as the excess of the consideration paid over the net amounts of assets and liabilities acquired from the target business. See the author's *Business Combinations and Consolidations* course for more information about how goodwill is initially recognized.

> **Commentary:** There was a time when the FASB considered charging goodwill to expense, rather than recognizing it as an asset. It stated that "this approach does not have strong conceptual merit, because goodwill meets the definition of an asset, which should not be written off unless it is deemed to be impaired."

The Nature of Goodwill Impairment

A publicly-held company is not allowed to *amortize* the goodwill asset (though privately held companies and nonprofit entities can do so, as discussed later). This differs from the depreciation applied to fixed assets, which gradually reduces their *carrying amounts* over time. Instead, the goodwill asset is reduced only when it is considered to be impaired, which is essentially when the value associated with an acquired entity begins to decline.

Goodwill is *impaired* when its carrying amount (the amount at which it is recorded on the books) exceeds its fair value. The fair value of goodwill cannot be measured directly; instead, you must back into this figure, measuring it as a residual value. The fair value of goodwill is only an estimate of the value of goodwill, and is only used to measure whether the goodwill asset has been impaired.

Commentary: As part of its standards formulation work, the FASB recognized that many users of both nonpublic entity and public entity financial statements generally exclude goodwill impairment losses from their quantitative analyses, and often view the impairment loss as a qualitative indicator of the relative success of an acquisition.

The Nature of a Reporting Unit

Goodwill is tested at the level of the reporting unit, so it is useful to understand exactly what this is. A *reporting unit* is an operating segment or one level below an operating segment. An operating segment is a component of a public entity, and possesses the following characteristics:

- *Business activities*. It has business activities that can generate revenues and cause expenses to be incurred. This can include revenues and expenses generated by transactions with other operating segments of the same public entity. It can also include activities that do not yet include revenues, such as a start-up business. [**Note:** This means that an operating segment does not have to have a balance sheet]
- *Results reviewed*. The chief operating decision maker of the public entity regularly reviews its operating results, with the intent of assessing its performance and making decisions about allocating resources to it.
- *Financial results*. Financial results specific to it are available.

Note: Since a reporting unit may not have its own balance sheet, it may be necessary to assign assets and liabilities to it in order to conduct a goodwill impairment test.

Commentary: The FASB considered a proposed alternative that would have required an entity to test goodwill for impairment at a higher level than a reporting unit, but concluded that the reporting unit "is the appropriate level for testing, because it best reflects the way an entity is managed and it commonly is the level at which goodwill is allocated."

Generally, an operating segment has a manager who is accountable to the chief operating decision maker, and who maintains regular contact with that person, though it is also possible that the chief operating decision maker directly manages one or more operating segments.

If a company has a matrix form of organization, where some managers are responsible for geographic regions and others are responsible for products and services, the results of the products and services are considered to be operating segments.

Some parts of a business are not considered to be reportable business segments under the following circumstances:

- *Corporate overhead.* The corporate group does not usually earn outside revenues, and so is not considered a segment.
- *Post-retirement benefit plans.* A benefit plan can earn income from investments, but it has no operating activities, and so is not considered a segment.
- *One-time events.* If an otherwise insignificant segment has a one-time event that boosts it into the ranks of reportable segments, do not report it, since there is no long-term expectation for it to remain a reportable segment.

If there are operating segments that have similar economic characteristics, their results can be aggregated into a single operating segment, but only if they are similar in all of the following areas:

- The nature of their products and services
- The nature of their systems of production
- The nature of their regulatory environments (if applicable)
- Their types of customers
- Their distribution systems

The decision to aggregate operating segments is based on the facts and circumstances, and so is more of a qualitative decision than a quantitative one.

In short, the nature of a reporting unit will depend on how an acquired entity is integrated into the operations of the acquirer, or – if the acquirer elects to keep it as a separate entity – how the acquirer subsequently structures the operations of the entity. Depending on the size and complexity of the business, a reporting unit could be identical to an operating segment, which might encompass the entire organization.

Overview of Goodwill Impairment Accounting

After goodwill has initially been recorded as an asset, do not amortize it (with the exception noted in the Goodwill Amortization section). Instead, test it for impairment at least once a year at the reporting unit level, as defined earlier. Impairment exists when the carrying amount of the goodwill is greater than its fair value.

The examination of goodwill for the possible existence of impairment involves a two-step process, which is comprised of a qualitative test, followed (if necessary) by a quantitative test. You can skip the first step and proceed directly to the second, but it is much less time-consuming to conduct the qualitative test first, which may allow you to skip the quantitative test entirely.

The two steps in the goodwill impairment testing process are noted in the following numbered list:

1. *Assess qualitative factors.* Review the situation to see if it is necessary to conduct further impairment testing, which is considered to be a likelihood of more than 50% that impairment has occurred, based on an assessment of relevant events and circumstances. Examples of relevant events and circumstances that make it more likely that impairment is present are as follows:

   - *Macroeconomic conditions deteriorate.* For example, there can be a decline in general economic conditions, greater difficulty in accessing funding, or significant fluctuations in foreign exchange rates. There may be other developments in the equity and credit markets that can also be considered a deterioration of these conditions.
   - *Industry deterioration.* For example, the level of competition increases, regulations become more stringent, or the market for the company's products declines.
   - *Costs increase.* For example, increases in the costs of labor and/or materials are resulting in a profitability and cash flow decline.
   - *Financial performance declines.* For example, actual results (in terms of cash flow, revenue, or earnings) decline below expectations, or decline in comparison to prior period results.
   - *Negative impact on reporting unit.* An event has occurred that impacts a reporting unit, such as the recognition of a goodwill impairment loss by a subsidiary, a change in the composition of its net assets, or an expectation that the unit will be sold.
   - *Share price decline.* There is a sustained drop in the price of the company's stock, either in relation to the share prices of peer entities or in absolute terms.
   - *Other items.* There may be turnover in the management team, the loss of key personnel, a pending bankruptcy, a change in customers, or the arrival of a lawsuit against the organization.

This list does not address all possible qualitative factors that could be assessed. You should consider other events and circumstances if they are relevant to the reporting unit under review.

This review is not entirely negative. You should also consider the impact of any positive events and circumstances that might mitigate the negative items on the preceding list.

> **Tip:** When reviewing these relevant events and circumstances, consider the extent to which they may impact how the unit's fair value compares to its carrying amount, and give greater weight to those items that have the greatest impact on the unit's fair value or the carrying amount of its assets.

> **Tip:** If the reporting unit has recently had its fair value calculated, you may include this valuation in your consideration of the difference between the unit's fair value and the carrying amount of its assets. For example, if the calculated fair value of a reporting unit was much greater than its carrying amount in the most recent test, it would take a substantial amount of negative evidence to offset this valuation. Conversely, only a slight excess of fair value in the most recent test would make any negative qualitative event a much more significant issue.

If the qualitative analysis indicates that the fair value of the reporting unit is more likely than not to exceed its carrying value, then you can terminate the impairment analysis. However, if impairment appears to be likely, continue with the second step in the impairment testing process. You can choose to bypass this step and proceed straight to the next step. If not, then stop here. If you do elect to bypass the first step, you can resume using this qualitative assessment for future impairment analyses.

2. *Identify potential impairment.* If step one indicates the possibility of goodwill impairment, or if you have chosen to bypass the first step entirely, then proceed to this step, which involves the quantitative calculation of the impairment amount. The essential task is to compare the fair value of the reporting unit to its carrying amount. If the fair value is greater than the carrying amount of the reporting unit, there is no goodwill impairment. If the carrying amount exceeds the fair value of the reporting unit, recognize an impairment loss in the amount of the difference, up to a maximum of the entire carrying amount (i.e., the carrying amount of goodwill can only be reduced to zero). You should consider the income tax effect from any tax-deductible goodwill on the carrying amount of the entity (or the reporting unit), if applicable, when measuring the goodwill impairment loss.

Once the goodwill impairment (if any) has been recognized, the newly-adjusted carrying amount of any remaining goodwill is its new accounting basis.

> **Note:** Once impairment of goodwill has been recorded, it cannot be reversed, even if the condition originally causing the impairment is no longer present.

These steps are illustrated in the following flowchart.

Goodwill Impairment Decision Steps

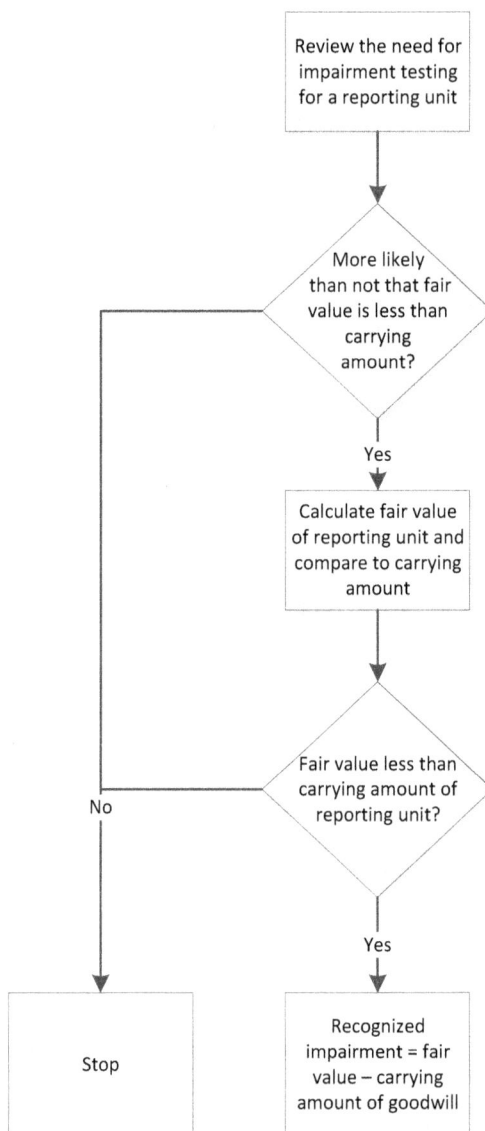

```
┌─────────────────┐
│ Review the need for
│ impairment testing
│ for a reporting unit
└─────────────────┘
          │
          ▼
      ◇ More likely
      than not that fair
      value is less than
      carrying
      amount? ◇
          │
         Yes
          │
          ▼
┌─────────────────┐
│ Calculate fair value
│ of reporting unit and
│ compare to carrying
│ amount
└─────────────────┘
          │
          ▼
      ◇ Fair value less than
      carrying amount of
      reporting unit? ◇
          │
         Yes
          │
          ▼
```

No

┌──────────┐   ┌─────────────────┐
│   │   │ Recognized   │
│ Stop   │   │ impairment = fair│
│   │   │ value − carrying │
│   │   │ amount of goodwill│
└──────────┘   └─────────────────┘

An essential part of this quantitative analysis portion of the impairment testing is the calculation of the reporting unit's fair value. The fair value of the reporting unit is assumed to be the price that the company would receive if it were to sell the unit in an orderly transaction (i.e., not a rushed sale) between market participants as of the measurement date. Other alternatives to the quoted market price for a reporting unit may be acceptable, such as a valuation based on multiples of earnings or revenue. A multiple of earnings or revenue might be an appropriate option when there are entities with comparable operations and economic characteristics to use as benchmarks. Of course, a multiple of earnings or revenue might not be appropriate when there are no such entities with a similar scope, nature, or size that can be used for comparison purposes.

> **Note:** An acquiring business can gain substantial value from any synergies and other benefits arising from its purchase of another business. This means that a measurement of the aggregated assets and liabilities of a reporting unit will likely differ from a measurement of the equity securities issued by that reporting entity. The difference is a *control premium* paid in order to gain a controlling interest over the reporting unit. This control premium may cause the reporting unit's fair value to be greater than its market capitalization. Thus, the quoted market price of the relevant equity security is not necessarily a good indicator of a reporting unit's fair value.

The following additional issues are associated with goodwill impairment testing:

- *Asset and liability assignment.* Assign acquired assets and liabilities to a reporting unit if they relate to the operations of the unit *and* they will be considered in the determination of reporting unit fair value. If these criteria can be met, even corporate-level assets and liabilities (such as pension obligations and environmental liabilities) can be assigned to a reporting unit. If some assets and liabilities could be assigned to multiple reporting units, assign them in a reasonable manner (such as an allocation based on the relative fair values of the reporting units), consistently applied.
- *Asset recognition.* It is not allowable to recognize an additional intangible asset as part of the process of evaluating goodwill impairment.
- *Goodwill assignment.* All of the goodwill acquired in a business combination must be assigned to one or several reporting units as of the acquisition date, and not shifted among the reporting units thereafter. The assignment should be in a reasonable and supportable manner, consistently applied. If goodwill is to be assigned to a reporting unit that has not been assigned any acquired assets or liabilities, the assignment could be based on the difference between the fair value of the reporting unit before and after the acquisition, which represents the improvement in value caused by goodwill.

> **Note:** Goodwill assignments to reporting units, as well as assignments of assets and liabilities to reporting units for goodwill impairment testing, do not have to be included in the financial reports for these reporting units.

- *Impairment estimation.* If it is probable that there is goodwill impairment and the amount can be reasonably estimated, despite the testing process not being complete when financial statements are issued, recognize the estimated amount of the impairment. The estimate should be adjusted to the final impairment amount in the following reporting period.
- *Reporting structure reorganization.* If a company reorganizes its reporting units, reassign assets and liabilities to the new reporting units based on a

reasonable methodology, consistently applied. Goodwill should be reassigned based on the relative fair values of the portions of the old reporting unit to be integrated into the new reporting units.

- *Reporting unit disposal.* If a reporting unit is disposed of, include the goodwill associated with that unit in determining any gain or loss on the transaction. If only a portion of a reporting unit is disposed of, associate some of the goodwill linked to the reporting unit to the portion being disposed of, based on the relative fair values of the portions being disposed of and retained. Then test the remaining amount of goodwill assigned to the residual portion of the reporting unit for impairment.

EXAMPLE

Armadillo Industries is selling off a portion of a reporting unit for $500,000. The remaining portion of the unit, which Armadillo is retaining, has a fair value of $1,500,000. Based on these values, 25% of the goodwill associated with the reporting unit should be included in the carrying amount of the portion being sold.

- *Reporting unit disposal, minority owner.* If a company has less than complete ownership of a reporting unit, attribute any impairment losses to the parent entity and the noncontrolling interest in the reporting unit on a rational basis. However, if the reporting unit includes goodwill that is attributable to the parent entity, then attribute the loss entirely to the parent, not the noncontrolling interest.
- *Subsidiary goodwill impairment testing.* Any goodwill recognized by a corporate subsidiary should be dealt with in the same manner described elsewhere in this section for the impairment of goodwill. If there is a goodwill impairment loss at the subsidiary level, then also test the reporting unit of which that subsidiary is a part for goodwill impairment, if the triggering event is more likely than not to have also reduced the fair value of that reporting unit below its carrying amount.
- *Tax deductible goodwill.* If the reporting unit under examination has tax-deductible goodwill, recognizing an impairment loss could trigger a change in deferred taxes that causes the carrying amount of the unit to immediately exceed its fair value when the impairment loss is recognized. In this situation, you should determine the impairment loss, as well as the related deferred tax effect.

    Goodwill is deductible for tax purposes for selected business combinations in some jurisdictions. In these locations, a deferred tax asset or liability is recorded as of the acquisition date, based on the difference between the book basis and the tax basis of the goodwill. When the reporting unit's goodwill is tax deductible, its impairment creates an impairment loop, because the decrease in the book value of the goodwill asset increases the deferred tax asset (or decreases the liability), so that the carrying amount of the reporting unit actually increases. However, there is no offsetting increase in the fair value of the reporting unit, so another impairment test could be triggered.

EXAMPLE

Creekside Industrial has goodwill from an acquisition in one of its reporting units. All of the goodwill allocated to that unit is tax deductible. On the date of the reporting unit's annual impairment test, the reporting unit had a $400,000 book value for its goodwill, which is tax deductible, as well as deferred tax assets of $200,000 that relate to the tax-deductible goodwill, and book value of $400,000 for all other net assets. The reporting unit is subject to a 21% tax rate. Creekside's controller estimates that the fair value of the reporting unit is $900,000.

	Carrying Amount	Fair Value	Preliminary Impairment	Preliminary Deferred Tax Adjustment	Carrying Amount after Preliminary Impairment
Goodwill	$400,000	$0	-$100,000	$0	$300,000
Deferred taxes	200,000	0	0	21,000	221,000
Other net assets	400,000	0	0	0	400,000
Total	$1,000,000	$900,000	-$100,000	$21,000	$921,000

In the preceding example, the carrying amount of the reporting unit right after the impairment charge is greater than its fair value by the increase in the deferred tax asset, calculated as 21% of the impairment charge. To resolve the circular nature of the carrying amount exceeding the fair value, the controller applies the following simultaneous equation:

[tax rate ÷ (1 − tax rate)] × (preliminary temporary difference) = deferred tax asset

Equation for this example:

[21% tax rate ÷ (1 − 21%)] × ($100,000 preliminary temporary difference)
= $26,582 deferred tax asset

This results in the following revised table:

	Carrying Amount	Fair Value	Preliminary Impairment	Adjustment for Equation	Carrying Amount after Impairment
Goodwill	$400,000	$0	-$100,000	-$26,582	$273,418
Deferred taxes	200,000	0	0	26,582	226,582
Other net assets	400,000	0	0	0	400,000
Total	$1,000,000	$900,000	-$100,000	$0	$900,000

Creekside would report a $126,582 goodwill impairment charge, against which is offset a $26,582 deferred tax benefit that is recognized in the income tax line item.

Note: If the impairment charge calculated using this equation were to exceed the total goodwill allocated to the reporting unit, the total amount of the impairment charge would be limited to the goodwill amount.

- *Unrecognized assets.* When evaluating goodwill impairment, you should also consider whether there are any significant unrecognized intangible assets.
- *Taxable transaction.* As part of the fair value estimation, determine whether the reporting unit could be bought or sold in a taxable or non-taxable transaction, since this affects its fair value. This is a judgment matter, depending on the relevant facts and circumstances, and will depend on the feasibility of the assumed transaction, whether there are any tax laws or regulations that would prevent it, and whether the transaction would maximize the value received by the seller for the reporting unit.

EXAMPLE

Entwhistle Electric is conducting a goodwill impairment test for one of its reporting units. The reporting unit has the following assets and liabilities:

- Net assets, not including goodwill and deferred income taxes, of $60,000, with a tax basis of $35,000
- Goodwill of $40,000
- Net deferred tax liabilities of $10,000

Entwhistle's CFO believes it is possible that the reporting unit could be sold in either a taxable or a nontaxable transaction. Entwhistle could sell the reporting unit for $80,000 in a nontaxable transaction, or for $90,000 in a taxable transaction. If it were to be sold in a nontaxable transaction, then Entwhistle would have a $0 current tax payable resulting from the sale. Assuming a tax rate of 21%, if the unit were to be sold in a taxable transaction, then Entwhistle would have a current tax payable from the sale of $11,550 [calculated as $90,000 sale price - $35,000 tax basis, multiplied by the 21% tax rate].

In its quantitative impairment test, Entwhistle concludes that the reporting unit would be sold in a nontaxable transaction, based on this evaluation of its expected after-tax proceeds:

	Nontaxable	Taxable
Gross proceeds (fair value)	$80,000	$90,000
Less: Taxes arising from transaction	0	-11,550
Value to Entwhistle	$80,000	$78,450

In the quantitative impairment test, Entwhistle would determine the carrying amount of the reporting unit as follows:

Net assets	$60,000
Goodwill	40,000
Deferred taxes	-10,000
Carrying value	$90,000

The goodwill that has been allocated to the reporting unit is considered to be impaired, because the $90,000 carrying value of the reporting unit is greater than its $80,000 fair value (assuming that it is sold in a nontaxable transaction).

In this case, the reporting unit must recognize a goodwill impairment loss of $10,000, which is the excess of its carrying amount over its fair value. This loss is valid, since the amount does not exceed the $40,000 of goodwill that has been allocated to the reporting unit.

EXAMPLE

Entwhistle Electric is conducting a goodwill impairment test on another of its reporting units. The reporting unit has the following assets and liabilities:

- Net assets, not including goodwill and deferred income taxes, of $120,000, with a tax basis of $70,000
- Goodwill of $80,000
- Net deferred tax liabilities of $20,000

Entwhistle's CFO believes it is possible that the reporting unit could be sold in either a taxable or a nontaxable transaction. Entwhistle could sell the reporting unit for $130,000 in a nontaxable transaction, or for $160,000 in a taxable transaction. If it were to be sold in a nontaxable transaction, then Entwhistle would have a $0 current tax payable resulting from the sale. Assuming a tax rate of 21%, if the unit were to be sold in a taxable transaction, then Entwhistle would have a current tax payable from the sale of $18,900 [calculated as $160,000 sale price - $70,000 tax basis, multiplied by 21% tax rate].

In its quantitative impairment test, Entwhistle concludes that the reporting unit would be sold in a taxable transaction, based on this evaluation of its expected after-tax proceeds:

	Nontaxable	Taxable
Gross proceeds (fair value)	$130,000	$160,000
Less: Taxes arising from transaction	0	-18,900
Value to Entwhistle	$130,000	$141,100

In the quantitative impairment test, Entwhistle would determine the carrying amount of the reporting unit as follows:

Net assets	$120,000
Goodwill	80,000
Deferred taxes	-20,000
Carrying value	$180,000

The goodwill that has been allocated to the reporting unit is considered to be impaired, because the $180,000 carrying value of the reporting unit is greater than its $141,100 fair value (assuming that it is sold in a taxable transaction).

In this case, the reporting unit must recognize a goodwill impairment loss of $38,900, which is the excess of its carrying amount over its fair value. This loss is valid, since its amount does not exceed the $80,000 of goodwill that has been allocated to the reporting unit.

Tip: From a practical perspective, it is almost always easier to estimate the fair value of the reporting unit based on a multiple of its earnings or revenues, though this should only be done when there are comparable operations whose fair values and related multiples are known, and which can therefore be used as the basis for a fair value estimate of the reporting unit.

Impairment testing is to be conducted at annual intervals. The impairment test may be conducted at any time of the year, provided that the test is conducted thereafter at the same time of the year. If the company is comprised of different reporting units, there is no need to test them all at the same time.

Tip: Each reporting unit is probably subject to a certain amount of seasonal activity. If so, select a period when activity levels are at their lowest to conduct impairment testing, so it does not conflict with other activities. Impairment testing should not coincide with the annual audit.

It may be necessary to conduct more frequent impairment testing if there is an event that makes it more likely than not that the fair value of a reporting unit has been reduced below its carrying amount. Examples of triggering events are a lawsuit, regulatory changes, the loss of key employees, and the expectation that a reporting unit will be sold.

> **Tip:** Private and non-profit entities only have to evaluate goodwill impairment triggering events as of the end of the reporting period. An entity that elects to take this approach does not have to monitor for goodwill impairment triggering events at other times. See the following section for more information.

The information used for an impairment test can be quite detailed. To improve the efficiency of the testing process, it is permissible to carry forward this information to the next year, as long as the following criteria have been met:

- There has been no significant change in the assets and liabilities comprising the reporting unit.
- There was a substantial excess of fair value over the carrying amount in the last impairment test.
- The likelihood of the fair value being less than the carrying amount is remote.

As an additional note for publicly-held companies that report segment information, the asset, liability, and goodwill allocations used for goodwill impairment testing do not have to be the same as the amounts stated in segment reports. However, aligning the two sets of information will make it easier to conduct both impairment testing and segment reporting.

Goodwill Amortization

The effort required to monitor the goodwill asset is considered to be excessive for private companies, while the usefulness of goodwill information is also considered to be limited. These concerns arose from input received from the FASB, where private companies stated that the recurring cost and complexity of calculating the fair value of a reporting unit was excessive. As a result, the FASB now allows different accounting guidance for goodwill between nonpublic entities and public entities, so that nonpublic entities can use a more cost-effective approach.

> **Commentary:** The FASB observed that many nonpublic entities and small public entities have fewer internal resources that are qualified to calculate the fair value of a reporting unit, and that they incur greater costs to test goodwill for impairment relative to their accounting department budgets, as compared to large public entities.

Consequently, a private company is allowed to amortize goodwill on a straight-line basis over a ten-year useful life; it is not permissible to amortize goodwill over a period of more than ten years. This is known as the accounting alternative. The entity may amortize goodwill over a shorter period if it can demonstrate that a shorter useful life is more appropriate. If an organization chooses to amortize goodwill, it must still test the goodwill asset for impairment at either the entity or reporting unit level. This test is triggered when there is an event that indicates a possible decline in the entity's or reporting unit's fair value to a point below its carrying amount. If an impairment loss is recognized, then any remaining carrying amount is to be amortized over its remaining useful life.

> **Commentary:** Interestingly, allowing the goodwill amortization option goes against an earlier finding by the FASB, which was that "the pattern of expense recognition often does not align with the economics of the goodwill recognized, because not all goodwill declines in value and because it is difficult to estimate a useful life and an appropriate amortization method for goodwill."

The amortization of goodwill will eventually reduce the carrying amount of an organization's goodwill asset so much that goodwill impairment will be quite unlikely, thereby reducing the need to spend time on such testing.

> **Note:** This goodwill amortization option is also available for non-profit entities.

Some stakeholders were concerned that the cost and complexity that private businesses and non-profit entities would have to undergo to evaluate triggering events and measure goodwill impairment *during* the reporting period would be excessive. Accordingly, the rules were changed, so there is an option to only perform this analysis at the end of the reporting period. For this rule, the reporting period can be an interim period or an annual period. If you elect to take this option, you are not required to monitor for goodwill impairment triggering events during the reporting period. Instead, you should evaluate the facts and circumstances as of the end of the reporting period to determine whether a triggering event exists, and (if so), whether it is more likely than not that the goodwill asset is impaired. If a private company or non-profit entity elects not to take the option to amortize goodwill, it can still only perform the triggering event evaluation at the end of the reporting period.

> **Note:** You cannot apply this guidance retroactively to interim periods for which annual financial statements have already been issued.

> **Tip:** Only evaluating triggering events at the end of a reporting period is highly recommended, since you can include it as a standard part of the closing activities, where sufficient staff time can be scheduled for it.

EXAMPLE

Medusa Medical amortizes its goodwill over 10 years, and also adopted the accounting alternative for a goodwill impairment triggering event evaluation, performing a goodwill impairment test only at the end of its annual reporting period. During its first quarter, Medusa lost a major customer, and managed to replace it in the third quarter, resulting in a return to its previously budgeted sales and profit levels by the end of its fiscal year. Since Medusa only tests for goodwill impairment at the end of its annual reporting period, it will likely conclude that no triggering event existed, so no further impairment testing would be required.

If Medusa had instead chosen to test for impairment whenever there was an impairment triggering event, it might have concluded in its first quarter that the loss of a major customer represented a goodwill impairment triggering event that required further impairment testing.

Goodwill Disclosures

A company that has recognized goodwill as an asset should disclose the following information in its financial statements:

Disclosures for Periods in Which a Balance Sheet is Presented

When there is a change in the carrying amount of goodwill in a reporting period, the following disclosures are required:

- The gross amount and accumulated impairment losses as of the beginning of the reporting period.
- The amount of any additional goodwill that was recognized during the period, not including any goodwill associated with a disposal group that, when it was acquired, meets the criteria to be classified as held-for-sale.
- Any adjustments triggered by the subsequent recognition of deferred tax assets during the reporting period.
- Any goodwill included in a disposal group that was classified as held-for-sale and goodwill derecognized during the period that was not previously reported in a disposal group that was classified as held-for-sale.
- Any impairment losses recognized during the reporting period.
- Any net exchange differences arising during the period.
- Any other changes in the carrying amounts that occurred during the period.
- The gross amount and accumulated impairment losses as of the end of the reporting period.

In addition, if the reporting entity is publicly-held, it will also have to report the preceding information for each reportable segment, as well as in total. These entities will also have to report any significant changes in how goodwill was allocated to each reportable segment.

If a business combination had just occurred prior to the reporting date, it is possible that goodwill had not yet been allocated to a specific reporting unit. If so, you must disclose the unallocated amount, as well as the reasons for not allocating it by the financial statement issuance date.

There may be cases in which a reporting unit has a zero or negative carrying amount. If so, you must disclose these units, along with the amount of goodwill allocated to each one. Further, you must disclose the reportable segment into which these reporting units are aggregated.

Disclosures of Goodwill Impairment Losses

When the entity recognizes a goodwill impairment loss, it must disclose all of the following information in the financial statement footnotes:

- The facts and circumstances associated with the loss
- The amount of the impairment loss
- The method used to determine the fair value of the entity or reporting unit[1]
- The method used to allocate the impairment loss to the individual amortizable units of goodwill
- The income statement line item into which the impairment loss is aggregated

Disclosures for the Accounting Alternative

If a private business elects to take the amortization alternative, then it is subject to a different set of disclosure requirements. When additions are made to the goodwill asset in a period when a balance sheet is presented, the following disclosures are required:

- The amount assigned to goodwill in aggregate, as well as by each major business combination, or by major acquisition if the reporting entity is a nonprofit, or by any reorganization that results in fresh-start reporting.
- The weighted-average amortization period, both in total and by major business combination, or by major acquisition if the reporting entity is a nonprofit, or by any reorganization that results in fresh-start reporting.

In addition, the reporting entity must disclose its use of a goodwill impairment triggering event evaluation as part of its reporting of significant accounting policies.

SAMPLE DISCLOSURE

Treadway Corporation has three reporting units with goodwill – Home Equipment, Business Equipment, and Government Equipment – and two reportable segments – Exercise and Health Monitoring. The Publishing reporting unit has a negative carrying amount.

---

[1] Whether based on the prices of comparable business units or nonprofit activities, a present value or other valuation technique, or a combination of these approaches

The changes in the carrying amount of goodwill for the year ended December 31, 20X5 are as follows:

(000s)	Exercise	Health Monitoring	Total
Balances as of January 1, 20X5			
Goodwill	$1,500	$1,100	$2,600
Accumulated impairment losses	0	-200	-200
	1,500	900	2,400
Goodwill acquired during the year	150	100	250
Impairment losses		-50	-50
Goodwill written off due to sale of business unit	-500	0	0
Balance as of December 31, 20X5			
Goodwill	1,150	950	2,100
Accumulated impairment losses	0	-250	-250
	$1,150	$700	$1,850

The Health Monitoring segment is tested for impairment in the third quarter, following the annual budgeting process. Because of an increase in competition in the company's key markets, operating profits and cash flows were lower than expected in the fourth quarter of the prior year and the first and second quarters of the current year. Based on that pattern, the profit forecast for the next three years was revised downward. In September, a goodwill impairment loss of $50,000 was recognized in the Health Monitoring reporting unit. The fair value of that reporting unit was estimated using the expected present value of future cash flows.

The Publishing unit, to which $250,000 of goodwill is allocated, had a negative carrying amount at year-end. This reporting unit is part of the Exercise segment.

Goodwill Presentation

There are specific presentation requirements for where goodwill-related information is to be included in the financial statements. Specifically, if there has been goodwill impairment, present the related losses in a separate line item in the income statement, positioned before the subtotal of income from continuing operations. If the goodwill is associated with a discontinued operation, then present the loss, net of taxes, in a line item in the discontinued operations section of the income statement.

If the organization engages in goodwill amortization, disclose the gross carrying amounts of goodwill, accumulated amortization, and accumulated impairment losses, as well as the aggregate amortization expense for the period. Also report any goodwill included in a disposal group that is classified as held-for-sale, and goodwill derecognized within the reporting period that was not previously reported in such a disposal group.

The amount of goodwill recorded on a firm's balance sheet can be substantial, so it is important to include these disclosures in the financials.

Summary

The amount of goodwill carried on the books of many entities is substantial, and its fair value can vary significantly from its book value. To ensure that the book value does not exceed fair value, it is necessary to conduct periodic goodwill impairment testing, as described in this manual.

The testing for goodwill impairment can be both time-consuming and expensive, so take full advantage of the option to avoid testing by reviewing qualitative factors to see if there is a low likelihood of impairment. In addition, if your organization is privately held or a non-profit, consider amortizing the goodwill asset over time, since this can reduce the book value sufficiently to avoid the risk of incurring an asset impairment at some point in the future.

Glossary

A

Amortization. The practice of spreading an intangible asset's cost over its useful life through periodic charges to expense.

B

Business combination. A transaction in which the acquirer obtains control of another business (the acquiree).

C

Carrying amount. The amount at which an asset or liability is recorded on the books.

Control premium. The amount that a buyer is willing to pay over the current market price in order to acquire a controlling interest in a target company.

G

Goodwill. The excess paid by an acquirer over the fair value of the acquired assets and liabilities.

I

Impairment. When the carrying amount of an asset exceeds its fair value.

R

Reporting unit. An operating segment or one level below an operating segment (which is a component of a public entity).

Index

www.ingramcontent.com/pod-product-compliance
Lightning Source LLC
Chambersburg PA
CBHW051431200326
41520CB00023B/7435